The Little of Kitchen stuff

by Amy Arnold, Kerry Agricole
and Roxanne Rutter
Illustrations by Mike Phillips

LITTLE BOOKS WITH BIG IDEAS

Published 2011 by A&C Black Publishers Limited
36 Soho Square, London W1D 3QY
www.acblack.com

ISBN 978-1-4081-4048-2

Text © Amy Arnold, Kerry Agricole and Roxanne Rutter
Illustrations © Mike Phillips
Cover photographs © Shutterstock, 2011

Printed in Great Britain by Latimer Trend & Company Limited

This book is produced using paper that is made from wood grown in
managed, sustainable forests. It is natural, renewable and recyclable.

The logging and manufacturing processes conform to the environmental
regulations of the country of origin.

**To see our full range of titles
visit www.acblack.com**

Contents

Introduction

The **Little Book of Kitchen Stuff** provides a range of exciting, accessible and fun activities – all using an everyday kitchen implement or two! This book is intended for all practitioners working with young, inquisitive learners within the EYFS and KS1, who could be in Pre-Schools, Nurseries and Schools or with Childminders or Carers at home.

You could use the ideas in this book as starting points for creating and developing your own activities, unique to your setting and individual children, or you could use the ideas to inspire thinking creatively about other uses of kitchen gadgets that will engage and excite children.

Why kitchen stuff?

Some kitchen utensils and implements will be familiar to most children, whether it's a spoon or a dishcloth. By using a wide range of kitchen utensils and implements you are providing opportunities to build on children's current experiences, as well as providing new experiences with more unusual kitchen gadgets, and the endless possibilities they can offer.

A large number of Early Years settings are struggling to find adequate funds to keep resources fresh, exciting, inviting and memorable for children. We hope that the low cost and ease of accessibility of kitchen utensils will make this book appealing, regardless of any budget constraints. Kitchen utensils can be obtained cheaply from pound shops and supermarkets. Scouring charity shops and car boot sales could be perfect for finding more unusual implements or obtaining implements for just a few pence. Giving them a wash in Milton or hot water and washing up liquid will ensure that they are clean and ready to go!

Inspiring and supporting learning and development

By using a range of kitchen implements, children will have rich and countless opportunities to predict, explore, test, investigate, reflect, assess and summarise through exciting and inspiring activities, both child-initiated and adult supported. Children will become more creative and confident to explore the full potential of everyday items, which they have probably only ever seen do one specific job e.g. mashing potatoes! There are no ceilings placed on children's learning or imagination, no right or wrong and no boundaries to inhibit or limit their learning. Nearly all of the kitchen implements in this book will certainly help children to develop hand-eye co-ordination along with developing fine motor skills and strength in their fingers, hands, wrists and forearms.

By providing opportunities for children to access and use a range of kitchen implements in their free flow play, they will have an open path of enquiry and discovery, which can be sensitively supported and facilitated by adults at an appropriate time.

An investigative area could house a changing selection of kitchen implements or a table top display featuring tea-towels, tablecloths and baskets of utensils could invite children to transport the implements to their desired area of learning and discovery. Regularly using kitchen implements in real, genuine and purposeful cooking activities will encourage and develop lifelong learning skills.

Throughout this book, the activities highlight some of the learning opportunities that could arise. These may well be different for individual children's unique learning journeys. Observing children engaged in the activities will ensure that you understand and consider their interests, development and learning.

Health and safety

Using kitchen implements can fuel great discussions on health and safety and managing risks. Some implements may be sharp or spiky; some may require a firm hand or positioning on a flat surface. Chatting with children, listening to and supporting their ideas on how to keep safe is a powerful way of helping children to assess and manage their own risks. Children need to feel confident to 'have a go' and embrace opportunities for new learning, comfortable that they have considered any risks involved both with, and more increasingly without, the support of an adult.

Home and setting links

We know that strengthening the links between the home and setting or school can be powerful in supporting children's learning and development, across all areas of learning. Ensuring that parents are aware of the endless learning opportunities through open-ended everyday resources, could open up a whole new world of play and discovery in their home environment.

Displaying photographs of the children actively exploring and discovering through using kitchen implements, along with captions of their thoughts or ideas and links to learning and development, will demonstrate the importance you place on open-ended discovery.

Children will be able to use their new knowledge and skills at home, building and extending on their learning within the setting. Using a variety of communication methods to keep parents regularly informed will help them to feel more involved and less likely to be surprised when their child wants to pour paint into a salad spinner!

A brush with the past!

Using a pastry brush to explore and uncover

What you need:

▶ Pictures or video clips of an archaeological dig

▶ A large tray or container such as, a builder's tray or potting tray. (Smaller trays such as seed or cat litter trays would work well too.)

▶ A selection of items to discover that could be linked to children's current interests or an interesting collection of items such as coins from different countries, small bottles or pieces of costume jewellery

▶ Fine sand to bury the items in

▶ Pastry brushes – both traditional fibre bristles and more recent silicone bristles

▶ Logs, pebbles, shells or miniature flags and signs to place on top of the sand (You could theme your sand scene with a shipwreck and barrels or dinosaurs and logs.)

I will need

What you do:

▶ **Explore and talk**

▷ Explore the different pastry brushes. What do they feel like? What could they be used for?

▷ Discuss the sand tray(s). What can you see?

▷ Introduce the children to the language and purpose of an archaeological dig. Show them pictures or video clips of digs taking place. Highlight how gentle and careful archaeologists are. I wonder why...

▷ Model the language relating to the passing of time e.g. past, old, a long time ago.

▶ **Investigate and experiment**

▷ Be archaeologists! I wonder if there is anything underneath the sand.

▷ Using the pastry brush, gently move sand away to uncover items or maybe just the bottom of the tray!

▷ Talk about the shape, size and colour of the mystery items as they are exposed.

▷ Where could they have come from? Are they old or new? How do we know? I wonder who they belonged to...

▷ Which brush works best? I wonder why...

Taking it further

▶ Bury just one or two items such as a sail from a boat and a small boot. Listen to children's ideas of where they came from, who they belong to, how they got there...

▶ Create a co-ordinates map with picture clues to represent where the items are buried. Model how to read a co-ordinates map. Help children to match the map to the sand tray and hunt for items.

▶ Devise a treasure hunt outside with picture clues for the children to follow and discover further hidden treasures.

And another idea...

▶ Try using pastry brushes for mark making with paints or water or in gloop, or 'dry' mark making patterns in flour, rice grains or lentils.

▶ Use pastry brushes to assist with minibeast hunts by gently brushing soil from logs.

▶ Create secret letters, numbers or messages using glue and glitter. Using a pastry brush, children can brush off the glitter to discover the secret!

▶ And of course...bake some delicious treats and use the brush for its original intended purpose!

Learning and development

▶ Respond in a variety of ways to what they see, hear, touch and feel. (CD: 40-60+ months)

▶ Use one-handed tools and equipment. (PD: 30-50 months)

▶ Handle tools and objects safely and with increasing control. (PD: 40-60+ months)

▶ Investigate objects and materials by using all of their senses as appropriate. (KUW: 40-60+ months)

▶ Begin to differentiate between past and present. (KUW: 40-60+ months)

▶ Extend their vocabulary, exploring the meanings and sounds of new words. (CLL: 40-60+ months)

Wash and scrub up!

Using familiar stories and rhymes as stimulus to predict, test and evaluate a variety of cleaning materials

What you need:

▶ A selection of cleaning materials e.g. cleaning cloths, scourers, wire wool pads, dish brushes

▶ Plastic bowls or plates (prepared with dried-on porridge)

▶ Spoons (prepared with dried-on porridge)

▶ Washing up bowl

▶ Washing up liquid

▶ Porridge (or other food source from familiar story or rhyme)

▶ Water or milk

What you do:

▶ **Explore and talk**

▷ Use a range of senses to explore the cleaning cloths and materials.

▷ Observe, listen and note as children describe the texture, pattern and smell of the materials. How do they handle them? Do they use any prior knowledge of the materials to model cleaning or scrubbing?

▶ **Investigate and experiment**

▷ Read the children a letter from The Three Bears:

Dear Little Fishes,

Please could you help us with a little problem? Goldilocks has left us with a terrible mess to clean up. We have lots of bowls and spoons that have dried porridge all over them. We don't know which cloth or brush would be best for cleaning the porridge off. We are too busy fixing beds and chairs to find out. Could you test them for us and let us know please.

Thank you very much

Love,

The Three Bears

▷ Encourage children to have a guess at which one they think will be best for cleaning off the porridge. Why do they think that? How could they find out? Which will be the quickest? Scrub the best?

▷ Using a sink or washing up bowl, experiment with different cleaning materials to clean off the dried porridge. Encourage children to talk about what they are doing: 'I need to scrub hard', 'It's not coming off' or 'The brush was brilliant.' Repeat back what the children have said so the rest of the group are involved in hearing each other's discoveries.

▷ Examine the bowls after cleaning and listen to the children share their thoughts and ideas.

▷ Ensure the children have an opportunity to test a few different cloths and brushes before summarising their ideas on which was best.

Taking it further

▶ Report back to the Three Bears, perhaps through drawings, messages on bear-shaped notepaper, photographs or a video recording.

▶ Use different sized bowls and spoons to support children's learning and development of size and scale.

▶ Extend the activity by introducing a wider challenge for the cloth materials: perhaps 'All the king's horses and all the king's men need help cleaning up the egg splats from Humpty Dumpty?' Or recite 'Pat-a-cake, pat-a-cake' after baking some real cakes and involve children in investigating the cleaning powers of a range of cleaning materials.

▶ Extend the collection by including a selection of brushes or cloths: dusters, face cloths, chamois leathers, patterned dish cloths, glasses cleaning cloths, muslin cloths and saddle cloths.

And another idea...

▶ Use scourers and sponges to create different landscapes in story boxes and small world play activities.

▶ Test the absorbency of different cleaning products. Which will suck up the puddle under Incy Wincy Spider's drainpipe the quickest?

▶ Explore the materials and textures using magnifying glasses or a microscope.

▶ Make sails for boats using dishcloths, sponges, scourers etc. Which will work best?

▶ Use everyday cleaning materials to create puppets of characters from stories. Wire wool pads could make fabulous space themed creatures!

▶ Introduce children to good early hygiene habits and encourage them to get involved in aspects of cleaning within the setting. Establish a simple system: e.g. red cloths are used for wiping tables and yellow cloths the floor.

Learning and development

▶ Display high levels of involvement in activities. (PSED: 40-60+ months)

▶ Form good relationships with adults and peers. (PSED: 40-60+ months)

▶ Explain own knowledge and ask appropriate questions of others. (KUW: 40-60+ months)

▶ Describe and talk about what they see. (KUW: 30-50 months)

▶ Look closely at similarities, differences, patterns and change. (KUW: 40-60+ months)

▶ Use talk to organise, sequence and clarify thinking. (CLL: 40-60+ months)

Funnel fun

This exciting activity encourages children's critical thinking. It develops rich language, estimation and prediction skills. Large funnels, small funnels, upside down funnels – fill them up and watch where your marbles roll to...

What you need:

▶ different sized funnels, plastic and silicone if obtainable

▶ string/washing line

▶ dried peas, marbles or sweets

What you do:

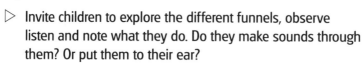

▶ **Explore and talk**

▷ Invite children to explore the different funnels, observe listen and note what they do. Do they make sounds through them? Or put them to their ear?

▷ Talk about funnels and their uses.

▷ Talk about what funnels are made of, why are they the shape they are?

▷ Invent new uses for funnels.

▶ **Investigate and experiment**

▷ Suspend the funnels using string or a washing line (preferably outdoors or in another large space).

▷ Children put peas (or marbles or sweets) into the funnels – where do they roll? Do they land in the same place? Whose travels the furthest? I wonder why?

Taking it further

▶ Change the height of the funnels and see what effect this has.

▶ Do different sized funnels change the results?

▶ Compare using different things such as peas, marbles, lentils and sweets

▶ Turn the funnels upside down – what happens?

▶ Record their findings using pictures, words and photos.

▶ Add drumsticks and use funnels to create sounds and music.

And another idea...

▶ Hang funnels over a water/sand tray/builder's tray. Children can pour in water/sand and investigate what happens.

▶ Make your own funnels/cones – small ones or even giant ones!

▶ Make a class investigation book to record activities and investigations to share with one another or parents and carers.

Learning and development

▶ Use own methods to work through a problem. (PSRN: 40-60+ months)

▶ Describe solutions to practical problems, drawing on experience, talking about own ideas, methods and choices. (PSRN: 40-60+ months)

▶ Work as part of a group, taking turns and sharing fairly. (PSRN: 40-60+ months)

▶ Say and use number names in order in familiar contexts. (PSRN: 40-60+ months)

▶ Begin to make patterns in their experience through linking cause and effect, sequencing, ordering and grouping. (CLL: 40-60+ months)

▶ Use talk to organise, sequence and clarify thinking and ideas. (CLL: 40-60+ months)

'Encourage children to tell each other what they have found out... This enables them to reflect upon their knowledge and to practice new vocabulary.' (DCSF, 2008)

All curled up

Using an ice cream scoop to explore and investigate the fascination of a curl!

What you need:

▶ An ice cream scoop

▶ Tub of ice cream

▶ Chocolate

▶ Grater

▶ Melon baller (for extending activity)

Allergy alert!

When handling foods items and if children are to enjoy eating their ice cream or chocolate curl creations, remember to double check for any allergies

What you do:

▶ **Explore and talk**

▷ Investigate the ice cream scoop. What is it? What could it be used for?

▷ Discuss and describe the shape of the scoop and handle. Has anyone seen one before? What was it being used for?

▶ **Investigate and experiment**

▷ Encourage children to use the scoop to serve ice cream – what happens? What shapes can they see?

▷ Experiment with and discuss the curl of the ice cream. Follow the children's directions and thoughts. Perhaps they want to create a bigger curl or smaller curl or maybe unravel the curl or dig really deep to see what happens.

▷ Stimulate children's thinking and communication skills by offering prompts such as: 'I wonder why it curls? What if it didn't curl? Where does the curl start?'

Taking it further

▶ Create curly toppings using chocolate and a grater – discuss the similarities and differences between the ice cream and chocolate curls.

▶ I wonder if all foods make a curl? Experiment with rice pudding or jelly.

▶ Look closely at a melon baller. Encourage children to predict what might happen when serving the ice cream with it.

▶ Investigate the shapes created by the melon baller. Are they the same as the scoop? What's different? I wonder why...

And another idea...

▶ Introduce ice cream scoops into a builder's yard small world play scene. Children can enjoy scooping and transporting sand, gravel, pebbles, bark chippings and other builder's yard materials.

▶ Look at curls and spirals in animals. Using the Internet find out about animals with curls or spirals e.g. snails or poodles!

▶ Experiment with curling ribbon around cylindrical blocks, pencils, water bottles or chair legs. How could you make a big curl? Tiny curl? Long curl?

▶ Select a small item to hide underneath the scoop. Describe the item to a partner e.g. 'It has spikes on its back. It's green.' Lift handle to reveal item, either when children have guessed or after a given amount of time or number of clues, 'Yes! It's a dinosaur!'

▶ Include ice cream scoops in the potting shed to fill pots with compost or to create spaces to plant bulbs indoors or outdoors.

Learning and development

▶ Use all of their senses to investigate objects and materials. (KUW: 40-60+ months)

▶ Look closely at similarities, differences, patterns and change. (KUW: 40-60+ months)

▶ Ask questions (about why things happen and how things work. (KUW: 40-60+ months)

▶ Describe and talk about what they see. (KUW: 30-50 months)

▶ Explain own knowledge and understanding, and ask appropriate questions of others. (KUW: 40-60+ months)

▶ Show an awareness of change. (KUW: 40-60+ months)

All in a spin!

Using a salad spinner to help Squirrel to sort his food pile

What you need:

▶ A handwritten letter from Squirrel asking for suggestions on how to sort his food pile.

▶ Dried pulses and beans in a variety of sizes e.g. chick peas, butter beans, split peas, pearl barley

▶ Sorting bowls and trays

▶ Salad spinner

▶ Squirrel puppet/toy

After setting the scene with autumn based stories, such as 'After the Storm' by Nick Butterworth and 'Scaredy Squirrel' by Melanie Watts, produce a letter that has arrived from Squirrel asking for ideas on how he could sort his winter food pile.

What you do:

▶ **Explore and talk**

▷ Arrange the bowls of mixed pulses and beans, sorting bowls, sorting trays, salad spinner and Squirrel on a table.

▷ Allow the children time to independently explore the objects. Observe, listen and note their individual observations, ideas and explorations.

▷ Talk about the items on the table. Have they seen any of them before? Where? What were they used for?

▷ Why do animals create food piles over the winter? I wonder where they keep them? What if they didn't make a food pile or another animal found their food pile?

▶ **Investigate and experiment**

▷ Recap Squirrel's letter to reiterate what help he needs.

▷ Enthuse and delight as children explore and investigate different ways of sorting, including using the salad spinner. 'Wow! What has happened? Are they sorted? I wonder how the spinner has sorted them?'

▷ Reinforce and facilitate language development as children explore tipping, filling and transporting the pulses and beans.

▷ Promote the language of size, colour and shape as children discuss their sorting, 'I've got all the small orange ones for Squirrel'.

▷ Experiment and discover the feel and sound of spinning with different quantities. 'What happens with a basket nearly empty or completely full? How could we make the very full basket spin?'

Taking it further

▶ Record a video message for Squirrel to tell him how you have sorted his food pile.

▶ Photograph individual children's sorting and annotate with an explanation of their sorting methods.

▶ Introduce balance scales and other woodland animals to create food piles for. Has rabbit got more than mouse? How could we find out?

And another idea...

▶ Use the pulses and beans to make patterns and pictures.

▶ Create unique and individual patterns and shapes by using paper/card and paint in the spinner – superb for firework explosions or Elmer the elephant patterns!

▶ Spin a story. Put in small items or pictures, for example a feather, a toy beetle, a jewel, a spoon and so on. Model pulling out an item and telling the story of where it came from. Can children select an item and tell a story based on the item?

▶ Spin a sound. Fill the spinner with foam letters. Encourage children to spin the salad spinner and then pick out a letter! Can they identify that letter? Is it in their name? What else starts with that letter?

▶ Experiment with mixing different materials such as shaving foam, food colouring and glitter. What happens? What other materials could be mixed?

▶ Grow some very simple salad leaves, pick them, wash them and spin them dry! Then create a delicious sandwich.

Learning and development

▶ Use developing mathematical ideas and methods to solve practical problems. (PSRN: 40-60+ months)

▶ Sort familiar objects to identify their similarities and differences, making choices and justifying decisions. (PSRN: 40-60+ months)

▶ Describe solutions to practical problems, drawing on experience, talking about own ideas, methods and choices. (PSRN: 40-60+ months)

▶ Look closely at similarities, patterns and change. (KUW: 40-60+ months)

Just a spoonful

Large spoons, small spoons, spoons with holes in, deep spoons, shallow spoons, spoons that hold a lot or a little!

What you need:

▶ Selection of different sized/shaped spoons – teaspoons, ladles, draining spoons, tablespoons, wooden spoons

▶ Dry coloured sand

▶ Containers – buckets, bowls, ice cream containers

▶ Feely bag

What you do:

▶ **Explore and talk**

  ▷ Invite and encourage children to explore the different spoons.

  ▷ Talk about spoons they have at home, spoons for different purposes and spoons that story characters might use such as Goldilocks or Meg the witch.

► **Investigate and experiment**
  ▷ Each child selects a spoon from the feely bag.
  ▷ Children can swap spoons and try again.
  ▷ They race to fill a container with sand only using the spoon they have selected. How long will it take to fill the container? How many spoonfuls can be added in a given time? Which spoon is quickest to fill the container?
  ▷ Encourage the children to express ideas, predict, question, investigate and discuss what happened and why things happened.

Taking it further

► Children can work with a partner who could count/record how many spoonfuls are needed to fill the containers.
► Try using a timer.
► Try using water, lentils, flour or salt instead of sand.

And another idea...

► Make a treasure basket collection of spoons: old and new, different shapes and sizes, spoons made from different materials – metal, plastic and silicone.

► Decorate spoons to create characters or families to use for small world play, role-play or storytelling.

Learning and development

► Use talk to connect ideas, explain what is happening and anticipate what might happen next. (CLL: 30-50 months)
► Use some number names accurately in play. (PSRN: 30-50 months)
► Show an interest in number problems. (PRSN: 30-50 months)
► Use own methods to work through a problem. (PSRN: 40-60+ months)
► Say and use number names in order in familiar contexts. (PSRN: 40-60+ months)
► Work as part of a group, taking turns and sharing fairly. (PSED: 40-60+ months)
► Use talk to organise, sequence and clarify thinking and ideas. (CLL: 40-60+ months)
► Ask questions about why things happen and how things work. (KUW: 40-60+ months)

Alien jelly monsters

Create wibbly wobbly jelly aliens using jelly moulds. Add features to make your alien come to life. Is he friendly? Is he scary? What planet does he come from?

What you need:

▶ Different sized jelly moulds

▶ Jelly (blocks/crystals/powder) of different flavours

▶ Jugs and spoons

▶ Things to decorate the jelly aliens such as googly eyes, string/wool, feathers, twigs, lollipop sticks, sequins and ribbon

What you do:

▶ **Explore and talk**

▷ Talk to the children about jelly. How do you make it? Why is jelly so wobbly? What is your favourite flavour? How does it taste/smell?

▷ Have you ever touched jelly? What does it feel like?

▷ Could we make something out of jelly? How about jelly monsters?

▷ Children share their ideas about what sort of monster they would like to create.

▶ **Investigate and experiment**

▷ Make the jelly with the children and pour into moulds. Refrigerate. You could appoint a 'jelly tester' to check when the jelly has set.

▷ Once set, the jelly can be emptied out of the moulds.

▷ Children can select items to decorate their own alien or work with a friend to create an alien together, negotiating what their alien should look like.

And another idea...

▶ Fill a container with jelly for children to explore.

▶ Make a jelly planet and add model alien monsters.

▶ Use jelly moulds in the sand tray with wet sand, gloop, shaving foam, play dough and salt dough.

Learning and development

▶ Show an awareness of change. (KUW: 40-60+ months)

▶ Talk about personal intentions, describing what they were trying to do. (CD: 40-60+ months)

▶ Maintain attention and concentration. (PSED: 40-60+ months)

▶ Interact with others, negotiating plans and activities and taking turns in conversation. (CLL: 40-60+ months)

▶ Talk activities through, reflecting and modifying what they are doing. (CLL: 30-50 months)

▶ Use language to imagine and recreate roles and experiences. (CLL: 40-60+ months)

▶ Respond in a variety of ways to what they see, hear, smell, touch and feel. (CLL: 40-60+ months)

Serving up a song

Use a large serving spoon or ladle to 'serve up a song'

What you need:

- Large bowl, bucket or plant pot
- A variety of small objects to represent songs and rhymes
- A serving spoon or ladle

A few ideas of objects which could represent songs:

- Small mouse – Hickory Dickory Dock
- Spider – Incy Wincy Spider
- Duck – Five Little Ducks
- Frog – Five Speckled Frogs
- Farmyard animals – Old MacDonald had a Farm

What you do:

▶ **Explore and talk**

▷ Share the bowl and some of the objects inside with the children. Name, describe and discuss the objects. What could we use them for?

▷ Introduce the idea of serving and show the children a range of implements that could be used for serving e.g. ladles, serving spoons or tongs. Share children's prior experiences of seeing serving in action.

▷ Serve up a song! Encourage children to use a serving implement to scoop up a song prop from the bowl. Help children to make links to a song the object could represent. 'Wow! Timmy has served up a pig... 'Old MacDonald had a Farm!'

▷ Together, sing and share the song.

Taking it further

▶ What other items could we put in the bowl to help us serve a song? Encourage the children to keep their eyes peeled for other items either from familiar songs or a song they have created, that could be added to 'serve up a song'.

▶ Use laminated photographs of the children (perhaps attached to small blocks for extra stability and ease of serving) and serve them up for songs with individual children identified such as 'Five Currant Buns – along came Bobby with a penny one day!'

And another idea...

▶ Use a ladle or serving spoon to collect a portion of items, such as pebbles, split peas, pasta or glass nuggets. Discuss and predict the quantity, describe the weight and capacity. How many pebbles can you serve? Can anyone collect more than 5 in one spoonful?

▶ Create a story prop sack or box for 'The Magic Porridge Pot' or 'Stone Soup'.

▶ Enjoy using ladles and serving spoons to transport liquids e.g. a witch's brew could be created with green food colouring, water and small minibeast toys. Serve it up into picnic bowls or cups. Use the ladle for stirring and creating magic spells, make links to familiar stories such as 'Meg and Mog' by Jan Pienowski.

Learning and development

▶ Begin to build a repertoire of songs and dances. (CD: 40-60+ months)

▶ Make comparisons and create new connections. (CD: 40-60+ months)

▶ Explain own knowledge and understanding, and ask appropriate questions of others. (KUW: 40-60+ months)

▶ Say and use number names in order in familiar contexts. (PSRN: 40-60+ months)

▶ Use talk to give new meanings to objects and action, treating them as symbols for other things. (CLL: 30-50 months)

▶ Listen with enjoyment, and respond to stories, songs and other music, rhymes and poems and make up their own stories, songs, rhymes and poems. (CLL: 40-60+ months)

Crush, grind and crumble

Strengthening little hands and wrists whilst exploring changes in a range of items

What you need:

- ▶ Pestle and mortar
- ▶ Blindfold
- ▶ Items to make alternative pestle and mortars e.g. plastic bowls and small rolling pins
- ▶ Items to grind:
  - ▷ Cream Crackers, peppercorns, breakfast cereals, hundreds and thousands, salt, cinnamon sticks, coffee beans or a variety of herbs such as basil, rosemary or mint
- ▶ Photos or video clips of a pestle and mortar in use

What you do:

▶ **Explore and talk**

▷ Discuss the pestle and mortar and alternative items that could also be used to perform the same task. What could you do with them? What do the children instinctively do with them? Introduce children to the name of the item!

▷ If using a heavy pestle and mortar, use the opportunity to reinforce language of weight and lifting, as well as a health and safety reminder to keep fingers and toes safe!

▷ Using photographs or clips from the internet, discuss the function of a pestle and mortar. Who might use them? I wonder what they could be used for?

▷ Talk about the different items for grinding – allow children to use their senses to explore them. Listen to their descriptions and thoughts on the smell, texture and shape of the items along with their unique preferences and experiences.

▷ Explore foods before and after grinding e.g. coffee beans and ground coffee. Use photographs of cocoa beans and compare with cocoa powder.

▷ Model and develop new language such as grind, crush, mix, powder, crumble and bash.

▶ **Investigate and experiment**

▷ Use the pestle and mortars to bash, crush, grind!

▷ What happens to the items? How have they changed?

▷ What different smells are released? 'It smells like... It makes me think of... I don't like the smell of... My favourite smell is...'

▷ Can the crackers be changed back to how they were? Why not?

▷ Working with a partner or in small groups, blindfold one person, whilst the other chooses an item to grind. Can your partner guess the item? How did they know? Because of the smell or texture?

Taking it further

▶ Use a pestle and mortar to alter ingredients for cooking activities such as grinding herbs for breads or pizzas.

▶ Create small scent bags as gifts or for sensory props for stories and rhymes by grinding lavender, cloves or lemon grass – the list is endless!

▶ Use the outdoor environment to find items to create natural pestle and mortars, such as large stones and logs.

And another idea...

▶ Make potions or superhero power powder!

▶ Create perfumes using flowers and leaves which children find in the natural environment.

▶ Select materials from the environment to explore what happens when crushed e.g. chalk, crayons, dried sticks or leaves?

▶ Create collages and pictures using crushed materials. Mix together sand and shells for beach scenes or bark and leaves for forest scenes.

▶ Create rhymes, raps and jingles to accompany the actions of mixing and grinding.

Learning and development

▶ Describe and talk about what they see. (KUW: 30-50 months)

▶ Investigate objects and materials by using all of their senses as appropriate. (KUW: 40-60+ months)

▶ Look closely at similarities, differences, patterns and change. (KUW: 40-60+ months)

▶ Ask questions about why things happen and how things work. (KUW: 40-60+ months)

▶ Show an awareness of change. (KUW: 40-60+ months)

▶ Show an interest in different occupations – Chefs! (KUW: 30-50 months)

Fish slice fairytales

By hanging collected objects from it and using it as a mobile, a fish slice can be used as a great aid to help children sequence and re-tell some of their favourite stories

What you need:

▶ A fish slice (one per child or per group)

▶ Selection of ribbon and string

▶ Very small story props – children could create their own, which could be laminated and hole punched or very small props such as Christmas decorations, cake decorations or small world play items could be used.

▶ Stories which the children are familiar with or may be linked to a theme they have shown an interest in.

What you do:

▶ **Explore and talk**

▷ Listen as children share their thoughts and ideas about the story they have selected.

▷ Do they have a favourite character or part of the story? Why is it their favourite?

▷ Share the story together modelling and demonstrating the language of story sequencing: Beginning, next, after that...

▶ **Investigate and experiment**

▷ Model using some of the props (both collected and made) to tell a story familiar to the children.

▷ What could we use to help us tell your story?

▷ What happens in the beginning? E.g. with Cinderella: How could we make a small broom? (Try using twigs and raffia). Is there a small broom in our collection of things?

▷ Investigate how the broom could be attached to the fish slice.

▷ Wow! How does your story start? I wonder what happens next. Continue using or making props to create a visual display of a child's story and attaching them to the fish slice. You could use either a story they have created or a familiar one.

▷ Hanging from the Cinderella story fish slice mobile could be: a small broom (laminated pictures or mini object), a wand, a pumpkin (cake toppers and decorations around Halloween time are perfect), a small shoe and a wedding bell (little cake decorations are perfect for these).

▷ Or the story 'Sharing a Shell' might inspire children to paint and glitter their own sparkly sea creatures which could be laminated and hole punched. Added to these could be flowing seaweed or hanging pebbles and shells. How will the story unfold?

Taking it further

▶ Children could select their own items and create their very own tale. Small world characters from children's popular culture (often available on the front of magazines), along with scenery and props could be used to promote storytelling. Your very own Toy Story adventure or BEN 10 mystery to share!

And another idea...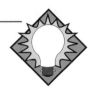

▶ Make hanging rhymes such as Hey Diddle Diddle or Twinkle Twinkle Little Star. Christmas tree decorations (always in the January sales!) can be just perfect for finding a small fiddle or range of stars.

▶ Create shape, pattern or number collections.

▶ Children select a large number to hang from their fish slice. What could four be? Can they find anything to represent that number? Maybe, a dog with four legs or a car with four wheels?

▶ Create collections to support topics or themes, or as part of an investigation area. Hanging the collections at child height gives children a different perspective on items. Collections could include: shells, twigs, autumn leaves and conkers, stars or fabrics.

Learning and development

▶ Show an understanding of the elements of stories, such as main character, sequence of events and openings. (CLL: 40-60+ months)

▶ Use vocabulary and forms of speech that are increasingly influenced by their experience of books. (CLL: 40-60+ months)

▶ Listen with enjoyment and respond to stories, rhymes and poems and make up their own stories, rhymes and poems. (CLL: 40-60+ months)

▶ Use talk to organise, sequence and clarify thinking, ideas, feelings and events. (CLL: 40-60+ months)

▶ Handle tools, objects, construction and malleable materials safely and with increasing control. (PD: 40-60+ months)

Icing bag snail trails

Making trails along hedges, up trees, along fences, through plants and undergrowth

What you need:

▶ Salt dough snails (children can make their own –
   see the recipe for making salt dough on page 80)

▶ Icing bags and tools

▶ Sparkly cornflour icing/gloop (see recipe on page 80)

▶ Outdoor area or garden scene in a builder's tray

What you do:

▶ **Explore and talk**

▷ Talk about snails and the trails that they leave. How could we make a snail trail? What materials could we use to make a slimy, gooey trail?

▷ How can we make icing? What do we need? Talk about icing tools and how they can be used.

▷ Children explore making gooey icing and other mixtures and test them out using different icing tools.

▶ **Investigate and experiment**

▷ Children make salt dough snails and then paint and decorate them.

▷ Adults create snail trails, using icing bags and gloop, for the children to follow and find snails at the end.

▷ Children use the icing bags filled with icing to create their own snail trails. They can hide snails at the end of their trail so their friends can follow the trails to find the snails.

Taking it further

▶ Children can add signs/captions/directions along the trails such as 'turn right here', 'this way', 'up and over', 'round the tree', 'way out'.

▶ Extend experience and learning through:

▷ finding out about snails

▷ making maps

▷ storytelling and writing

And another idea...

▶ Collect real snails to observe and even have a snail race! Remind children about returning them to the natural habitat afterwards.

▶ Look at other minibeasts such as spiders and create an icing spider web (perfect for Halloween!).

▶ Use icing tools to create shiny, sparkly pictures.

▶ Create a large collaborative snail complete with finger painting spirals – wonderful for building strength in little fingers!

Learning and development

▶ Show curiosity and interest in the features of objects and living things. (KUW: 30-50 months)

▶ Maintain attention and concentration. (PSED: 40-60+ months)

▶ Use language to imagine and recreate roles and experiences. (CLL: 40-60+ months)

▶ Extend their vocabulary, exploring the meaning and sounds of new words. (CLL: 40-60+ months)

▶ Find out about, and identify, some features of living things, objects and events they observe. (KUW: 40-60+ months)

▶ Respond in a variety of ways to what they see, hear, smell touch and feel. (CD: 40-60+ months)

'Active learning involves other people, objects, ideas and events that engage and involve children for sustained periods.' (DCSF, 2008)

A helping hand

Using kitchen gloves or rubber gloves to create colourful frozen hands

What you need:

- ▶ Kitchen gloves, rubber gloves or disposable gloves
- ▶ Food colouring
- ▶ Jug
- ▶ Water
- ▶ Access to a freezer
- ▶ Elastic bands

What you do:

- ▶ **Explore and talk**
    - ▷ Talk about kitchen gloves. How do you put them on? What do they feel like? What do they smell like? Are they the same as the gloves we wear when it's cold? What's the difference?

▷ Talk with the children about gloves. When do they wear them? Does anyone else in their family wear them? Have they seen rubber gloves before?

▶ **Investigate and experiment**

▷ Encourage children to add a few drops of food colouring to a jug of water. What happens? Prompt children to use words to describe what they can see e.g. cloudy, swirl, darker, smoky.

▷ Work together to collaboratively solve the problem of how to hold the glove and fill it with the coloured water.

▷ With adult support, secure the elastic band to the opening of the glove to prevent the coloured water leaking out.

▷ Discuss what might happen if the glove was put in the freezer.

▷ Carefully place the glove in the freezer. When the hand is frozen, together with the help of the children, carefully cut away the rubber glove. Listen, observe and note their reactions, comments and observations.

▷ Place the frozen hand in a glass dish or clear tray so children can fully observe the changes over a period of time.

Taking it further

▶ Photograph the frozen hand over a period of time. Can the children place the photos in order and describe what is happening?

▶ Create a hand in advance and leave for children to discover one morning. What is it? Where did it come from?

▶ What other frozen shapes could you create?

▶ Can the children make a story about the frozen hand? Perhaps a blue hand which belongs to Jack Frost or maybe a green hand which Shrek left behind?

▶ Measure how long the hand takes to melt. What happens to the shape? How does it change?

▶ Predict which parts will melt first – fingers or hand?

▶ Investigate reversible changes. Predict if the water could be frozen again. How long would it take?

And another idea...

▶ Race the clock! Wearing rubber gloves, how many small items, from pebbles to feathers, can you pick up and place in a tub in one minute? What is the smallest item you can pick up – pasta tube, sequin?

▶ Include rubber gloves throughout the outdoor area. Observe and note how children use them e.g. Does a pink pair of rubber gloves encourage children who were perhaps reluctant to use the digging area? Are children more confident about handling worms or other minibeasts if they're wearing gloves?

▶ Help Cinderella with a request to make her housework more fun! Create a glitzy, sparkly pair of gloves for her!

▶ Udder fun! A great way to find out about farm animals or food sources. Pierce one or two fingers of the rubber glove with a needle and hang upside down filled with milk or watered down white paint. Have a go at squeezing the udders to squirt out the milk!

Learning and development

▶ Describe and talk about what they see. (KUW 30-50 months)

▶ Investigate objects and materials by using all of their senses as appropriate. (KUW: 40-60+ months)

▶ Look closely at similarities, differences, patterns and change. (KUW: 40-60+ months)

▶ Ask questions about why things happen and how things work. (KUW: 40-60+ months)

▶ Show an awareness of change. (KUW 40-60 months)

Ice cube tray investigations

Young anthropologists can explore the ice age and discover creatures frozen in time!

What you need:

- ice cube trays
- coloured water
- small world play insects, spiders and snakes
- small leaves and foliage
- magnifying glasses
- tweezers

What you do:

▶ **Explore and talk**

▷ Explore and discuss ice cube trays of different sizes and shapes. How do we use them at home?

▷ Talk about ice – how it forms and why. Discuss how our earth was frozen during the ice age (children may be familiar with the recent films about the ice age).

▷ Could anything survive? What do things look like, feel like, smell like when they have been frozen?

▶ **Investigate and experiment**

▷ Using coloured water, prepare ice cubes with plastic insects, tiny pebbles or gems frozen inside.

▷ Empty the frozen trays and let the children watch the ice as it begins to melt and reveal creatures from the 'ice age'. They can use magnifying glasses to observe and tweezers to carefully extract the contents of the melting ice.

▷ Children can then select their own insects and creatures to freeze, placing them in ice cube trays.

▷ Mix small jugs of water with food colouring and gently pour over the insects.

▷ Place the trays in the freezer. Encourage the children to predict how long it will take for the water to freeze. Use a timer or a thermometer to measure the temperature. Together, record what happens.

▷ Once frozen, the ice trays can be emptied. The ice will begin to melt and reveal what is frozen inside!

Taking it further

▶ Try using other containers to create ice on a larger scale – yoghurt pots, dip containers or egg trays.

▶ Create an ice world in a builder's tray using bags of ice cubes and adding the insect filled cubes. Add glitter and sequins to create a magical scene.

▶ Add fragrances such as peppermint or lemon to extend the sensory experience.

And another idea...

▶ Use different shaped ice trays such as hearts, stars, strawberries and add fruity flavours to make mini ice lollies.

▶ Try setting jelly in ice trays and other containers for another sensory experience – link to the story 'Red Rockets and Rainbow Jelly' by Sue Heap and Nick Sharratt.

▶ Ice cube trays are also fantastic for problem solving, reasoning and numeracy activities – sorting, calculation and division.

Learning and development

▶ Use talk to connect ideas, explain what is happening and anticipate what might happen next. (CLL: 30-50 months)

▶ Use language to imagine and recreate roles and experiences. (CLL: 40-60+ months)

▶ Extend their vocabulary, exploring the meaning and sounds of new words. (CLL: 40-60+ months)

▶ Explain own knowledge and understanding, and ask appropriate questions of others. (KUW: 40-60+ months)

▶ Respond in a variety of ways to what they see, hear, smell touch and feel. (CD: 40-60+ months)

▶ Begin to differentiate between past and present. (KUW: 40-60+ months)

▶ Handle tools and objects safely and with increasing control. (PD: 40-60+ months)

Squeezy meat baster play

Having fun learning about distance, targets and measuring!

What you need:

- Meat basters
- Coloured glittery water
- Variety of liquids e.g. paint, washing up liquid, custard or soup in bowls or containers
- Plastic cups
- Chalk, hoop or masking tape
- Large sheets of paper/cardboard (optional)

What you do:

- **Explore and talk**

  ▷ Explore the meat basters with coloured glittery water inside. What will the children discover? How do they work? Can the water be moved? What happens if you squeeze it?

  ▷ Talk about the different liquids; encourage children to share their understanding of the liquids.

  ▷ Look carefully and describe the liquids, are they all the same? What do they look, smell and feel like?

▶ **Investigate and experiment**

▷ Use chalk, a hoop or masking tape to identify a 'squirting spot' – a spot to squirt the basters from.

▷ Place large sheets of paper in front of the spot, or alternatively use the playground! Squirt and then measure how far the liquids reach.

▷ Take it in turns to stand in the squirting spot and see how far different liquids can be squirted. Which liquid squirts the furthest? Are they easy to suck into the baster?

▷ Compare and discuss the patterns and shapes the different squirts make, how far they travel, where they land. Support and extend children's own unique fascinations with squirting.

Taking it further

▶ Can children chalk their name next to their squirt?

▶ Create a colour or number target for children to aim for.

▶ Measure the length of the squirts using footsteps, rope or builder's measuring tape.

And another idea...

▶ Create hanging targets for the children to aim at such as laminated ducks or numbered spiders.

▶ Make potions and use the meat basters to decant and fill different sized and shaped bottles and containers, with magic coloured potions.

Learning and development

▶ Sustain attentive listening, responding to what they have heard with relevant comments, questions or actions. (CLL: 40-60+ months)

▶ Begin to make patterns in their experience through linking cause and effect. (CLL: 40-60+ months)

▶ Investigate objects and materials by using all of their senses as appropriate. (KUW: 40-60+ months)

▶ Look closely at similarities, differences, patterns and change. (KUW: 40-60+ months)

▶ Ask questions about why things happen and how things work. (KUW: 40-60+ months)

Sieve and search

Sift 'under the sea' or 'down in the pond' to see what you can discover. Maybe a fish, slimy seaweed or even treasure!

What you need:

- ▶ water/sand tray or fish tank
- ▶ stones, pebbles and shells
- ▶ coloured sand
- ▶ weeds, plants and foliage
- ▶ small world resources (undersea/pond)
- ▶ treasure: gems, glass beads, sequins, coins, an old pocket watch, rings

What you do:

▶ **Explore and talk**

> ▷ Children can share experiences of visits to the seaside, crabbing or pond dipping. Talk about what you might find under the sea or down in the pond.

> ▷ Share stories about the seaside or pirate adventures.

▶ **Investigate and experiment**

> ▷ Create an undersea world or murky 'pond' with small world resources in a water tray.

▷ You could bury interesting objects, treasure, sea or pond creatures etc. under sand and stones.

▷ Children use sieves and tea strainers to search and discover what is buried 'under the sea' or 'down in the pond'.

Taking it further

▶ Add food colouring, glitter and sequins to the water creating different effects and moods.

▶ Create cloudy, murky, muddy water by adding soil, cornflour or jelly crystals.

▶ Try using dry sand, shredded paper, straw, compost or leaves and link to interests, current topic or theme.

And another idea...

▶ Add sieves and tea strainers to a treasure basket/box.

▶ Make storybooks about under the sea or down in the pond.

▶ Create artwork based on the children's discoveries when sifting and searching 'under the sea'.

Learning and development

▶ Show curiosity and interest in the features of objects. (KUW: 30-50 months)

▶ Describe and talk about what they see. (KUW: 30-50 months)

▶ Investigate objects and materials using all of the senses. (KUW: 40-60+ months)

▶ Interact with others, negotiating plans and activities and taking turns in conversation. (CLL: 40-60+ months)

▶ Use talk to connect ideas, explain what is happening and anticipate what might happen next. (CLL: 30-50 months)

▶ Extend their vocabulary, exploring the meaning and sounds of new words. (CLL: 40-60+ months)

▶ Use every day words to describe position. (CLL: 40-60+ months)

▶ Respond in a variety of ways to what they see, hear, smell, touch and feel. (CLL: 40-60+ months)

It's raining cats and dogs

Elephant's shower has broken, could we create him a new one?

What you need:

▶ Old or broken umbrellas – perhaps donated from parents

▶ Tools for making holes in the umbrella – scissors, hole puncher, skewers

▶ Watering cans, jugs, bottles or hoses

▶ Outdoor space and towels

Health & Safety Alert

Check umbrellas carefully for any sharp or dangerous prongs.

What you do:

▶ **Explore and talk**

  ▷ Have the children seen umbrellas in use before? Talk about an umbrella they have seen or used.

  ▷ How can the holes be made? What happens to the holes when the umbrella is open or closed? Do umbrellas normally have holes? Are all the holes the same shape or size?

  ▷ Predict what will happen now the umbrella has holes in it.

▶ **Investigate and experiment**

▷ Identify a shower spot! If you have all-in-one hooded outdoor suits, children could experience first hand the large scale sieve! Or use a large soft toy. What happens when water is poured onto the holey umbrella?

▷ Is anything different from using the small sieves in the water tray?

▷ Hang the umbrellas upside down and pour water into them. What happens? What does it feel like?

Taking it further

▶ Explore the effects of holding the umbrella at different heights.

▶ Look closely at any puddles that occur. Why and how are puddles made?

▶ Match movements to music 'We're singing in the rain'.

▶ Wear Wellington boots. Who can make the biggest splash?

▶ Use drainpipes, a watering can and a spider to play around with the rhyme 'Incy Wincy Spider'.

And another idea...

▶ Make holes in a range of bags – from a sandwich bag to a large carrier bag. Can we make the water squirt further? Can we stop the water coming out? Does it come out more quickly or slowly with bigger holes?

▶ Investigate what happens under the holey umbrella on a sunny day? Where do the patterns come from? Would you be safe from the sun under the umbrella?

Learning and development

▶ Investigate objects and materials by using all of their senses as appropriate. (KUW: 40-60+ months)

▶ Look closely at similarities, differences, patterns and change. (KUW: 40-60+ months)

▶ Ask questions about why things happen and how things work. (KUW: 40-60+ months)

▶ Work creatively on a large or small scale. (CD: 40-60+ months)

▶ Describe solutions to practical problems, drawing on experience, talking about own ideas, methods and choices. (PSRN: 40-60+ months)

Crazy hair!

Using a garlic press to create beards, luscious locks or other imaginative strands!

What you need:

▶ Garlic press
▶ Selection of cutters such as an angel, gingerbread man,
   Father Christmas, teddy bear, dinosaur, dog, cat, rabbit – anything
   where fur or hair can be added for effect
▶ Rolling pins
▶ Salt dough

What you do:

▶ **Explore and talk**

▷ Include a garlic press as a regular accessory for malleable materials and give children a chance to freely explore the full potential of creating strands.

▷ Experiment with adding different coloured play dough into the garlic press How do the colours join? Marvel in the multicoloured strands that can be created!

▷ Using sparkly play dough (add glitter) to make a spider's web or mermaid's tail.

▷ Talk about the variety of cutters. What can the children see? Which is their favourite? Why?

▶ **Investigate and experiment**

▷ Introduce the idea of making their very own salt dough figures. These could include a storybook character, animal or fantasy creatures. Help children to roll the salt dough and use their desired cutter shape.

▷ Do they need to add a beard? Or hair? If the children have independently used the garlic press they should be familiar with creating strands. If not, model and help the children use the garlic press to create salt dough hair!

▷ Gently position and push hair into place – much easier with smaller fingers!

▷ Use a flat implement to mark children's initials in the back before baking. It will save hours later!

▷ Bake the creations in an oven on a very low heat for several hours or leave to air dry for an extended period of time.

▷ Paint and decorate!

▷ Apply a coat of PVA glue (will dry clear) to prevent paint peeling.

Taking it further

▶ Create characters for popular storybooks such as a hairy, scruffy Gruffalo! Or maybe Three Billy Goat Gruffs? Instead of using cutters, sculpt 3D shapes such as three Owl Babies!

▶ Create decorated paper, wrap the decoration and attach ribbon as a gift for parents or carers. They could add a home made gift tag.

And another idea...

▶ Use biscuit dough (see recipe on page 80) to make birds' nests complete with little eggs (a real alternative to Shredded Wheat!).

▶ Experiment with squeezing different textures through the garlic press. What happens to jelly or shaving foam?

▶ Include a garlic press in soap flake mixture play, along with whisks and mashers.

▶ After using a garlic press, use a toothpick to clean out the individual holes – a real fine motor skill challenge!

Learning and development

▶ Explore colour, texture, shape, form and space in two or three dimensions. (CD: 40-60+ months)

▶ Experiment to create different textures. (CD: 40-60 months)

▶ Choose particular colours to use for a purpose. (CD: 40-60+ months)

▶ Talk about personal intentions, describing what they were trying to do. (CD: 40-60+ months)

▶ Use a range of small and large equipment. (PD: 40-60+ months)

▶ Be confident to try new activities, initiate ideas and speak in a familiar group. (PSED: 40-60+ months)

A mashing time

Using mashers to build the Three Little Pigs' houses

What you need:

▶ A collection of mashers
▶ Toolbox to hold mashers
▶ Shredded paper
▶ Flour and water paste
▶ Wood shavings
▶ Mud
▶ Straw

What you do:

▶ **Explore and talk**

▷ Read the story of The Three Little Pigs.

▷ Reveal your collection of papers, mud, straw. 'Oh no! We need to help the pigs rebuild their homes'. Ask the children to help you to rebuild the homes of the three little pigs. 'The trouble is...this is the only toolbox we have...'

▷ Reveal a toolbox with a selection of mashers. Listen to the children's ideas about how they could rebuild the houses. Encourage the children to think about mixing up a new mixture to create a pulp.

► **Investigate and experiment**

▷ Let the children make pulps by mashing together shredded paper – sand and flour and water paste for the brick house; mud, wood shavings and water for the stick house; and straw and water for the straw house.

▷ Encourage the children to predict which house will be the toughest. What is happening as they mash the pulp?

Taking it further

▶ Make small model houses for small world play. Add soft toy pigs or small world farm pigs to the houses for the children to recreate the story. Set the houses in a builder's tray and add sand at the base. Keep the storybook, puppets and additional props nearby.

▶ What if one morning we discover that two of the houses have blown over? What can we do? How could we make them stronger?

▶ Find a letter from one of the three little pigs, saying that they love their new house but they would like to have a window/door/garden? Can the children create a home with a window? A miniature garden?

And another idea...

▶ Have a collection of mashers available in the sand tray.

▶ Add mashers and washing up liquid or soap flakes to a water tray.

▶ Include mashers in the outdoor area. Do they help children to make mud pies? How do the children use them?

▶ Mash bananas for a snack or to include in a banana loaf or muffin recipe.

▶ Use mashers to make creations using play dough or clay.

▶ Compare the shape and size of holes in different mashers.

Learning and development

▶ Display high levels of involvement in activities. (PSED: 40-60+ months)

▶ Form good relationships with adults and peers. (PSED: 40-60+ months)

▶ Describe and talk about what they see. (KUW: 30-50 months)

▶ Explain own knowledge and understanding, and ask questions of others. (KUW: 40-60+ months)

▶ Use talk to organise, sequence and clarify thinking. (CLL: 40-60+ months)

▶ Use a range of small and large equipment. (CLL: 40-60+ months)

Great fun with a grater

Using graters to stimulate the senses and make soapy solutions

What you need:

▶ Selection of different soaps (baby soap, coal tar, shaped novelty soaps)

▶ Graters – box grater, stand up grater or small zester

▶ Water tray, builder's tray or cat litter tray (unused!)

▶ Dolls and plastic ducks

What you do:

▶ **Explore and talk**

▷ Give children plenty of time to explore the selection of soaps and packaging.

▷ Observe and note their comments and observations on the soaps. Do they have a preference? Record the language they use to describe the smells, colours and shapes.

▷ Share together existing knowledge of graters and observe, note and record how children communicate their prior experiences and understanding of graters.

▷ Reinforce the safety message of keeping fingers and knuckles well away from the grater when rubbing up and down.

► **Investigate and experiment**

▷ Lather up! In the water trays explore what happens when water is added to soap. Enjoy the sensation of creating lather and the challenge of holding on to a slippery soap.

▷ Promote children's language by encouraging and modelling words to describe the different aromas, textures, patterns and shapes that emerge from their explorations.

▷ What will happen if the soap is grated? Explore grating different soaps – you could try using smaller trays such as seed trays. What soapy mixture can you make? Can you make a new soap creation? Can we make bubbles? I wonder which soap makes the biggest bubbles?

▷ Follow the children's direction of learning as they explore and discover the magical world of lathers and bubbles. Will it lead to creating large bubbles outdoors or maybe washing all of the tables and chairs?

Taking it further

► Send correspondence to the children, giving them a real reason to create their own soapy mixes and get washing e.g.

▷ All the babies have been busy playing outside and are now very dirty. Could they be given a bath, ready for bedtime? Provide a baby bath and baby soap for children to grate and make their own lathery solution.

▷ A letter from Mother Duck: As you know my five little ducks went missing. They came back very smelly. Please could you wash them for me ready for our adventure in the big pond tomorrow? Five grubby ducks could be gathered outside!

► You could try grating soap and using containers or moulds to make new shapes and designs of soap!

► Link to stories such as: 'Mrs Mopple's Washing Line' by Anita Hewett and Robert Broomfield (Red Fox) or 'Mrs Lather's Laundry' by Allan Ahlberg (Puffin).

► Create an interactive display with items such as soap, graters, a selection of pegs, different style washing powders, washing up bowls, an old style washboard and non fiction texts such as 'I wonder why soap makes bubbles?' by Barbara Taylor (Kingfisher).

And another idea...

▶ Cover a grater with kitchen foil and create rubbings. Could they be dragon scales, fish scales or part of a mermaid's tail?

▶ Grate wax crayons that have become small and tricky to use. Place the shavings in a laminating sheet and laminate. Create wonderful window pictures to hang and display.

▶ Use the colours and patterns created from the laminating as inspiration for exploring different methods of mixing colours using heat. You could bake 'rainbow' buns using hundreds and thousands or food colouring as part of the mixture.

▶ Use soap gratings to make new shaped soaps, exploring the shapes and sizes of moulds.

Learning and development

▶ Talk about personal intentions, describing what they are trying to do. (CD: 40-60+ months)

▶ Respond to comments and questions, entering into dialogue about their creations. (CD: 40-60+ months)

▶ Respond in a variety of ways to what they see, hear, smell, touch and feel. (CD: 40-60+ months)

▶ Use simple tools to effect changes to materials. (PD: 40-60+ months)

▶ Practice some appropriate safety measures without direct supervision. (PD: 40-60+ months)

▶ Handle tools, objects and malleable materials safely and with increasing control. (PD: 40-60+ months)

Whisk up a storm

Using familiar songs and rhymes to explore circular mark making.

What you need:

► A collection of whisks

► Paints of various colours

► Glitters in various colours

► Builder's tray (Tuff spot)

► Aprons/protective clothing

► Metallic, glass or plastic bowls

What you do:

► **Explore and talk**

▷ Look at the whisks and ask the children what they are used for? Generate ideas of how whisks are used and ask children to model how they would use one.

▷ Comment and highlight on the spinning circular motion that the children make. As the children are swirling round sing 'Round and Round the Garden like a Teddy Bear'.

▷ Suggest how it would be fun to use the whisk to splatter paint and make a swirly picture. Can the children make the tracks of the teddy bear going round and round the garden?

► **Investigate and experiment**

▷ Encourage children to make large scale swirling patterns with their whisk in the builder's tray.

▷ Add paint and glitter and watch as the children make large scale movements winding and spreading the paint round and round. Take a print of the pattern by gently laying paper over the circular paint.

▷ Add a second paint colour, some glitter, water or bubble mixture.

▷ Try spinning the whisk in between two hands to make a splatter effect.

Taking it further

▶ Display the circular swirl patterns as celebrations of mark making.

▶ Use the whisk like an Indian singing bowl. Collect metallic bowls, glass bowls, plastic bowls and see if the whisks can make the bowls sing.

▶ Use the whisks to make music by swirling various materials (a bowl of conkers, a bowl of paper clips, a bowl of glass beads). How are the sounds different?

▶ Sing 'The Wheels on the Bus Go Round and Round', 'Wind the Bobbin Up', while making large hand movements.

▶ Take the circular mark making outside using watering cans on the playground.

And another idea...

▶ You could try adding whisks to the water tray with bubble mixture to make a foamy bath for the teddy bears.

Learning and development

▶ Display high levels of involvement in activities. (PSED: 40-60+ months)

▶ Form good relationships with adults and peers. (PSED: 40-60+ months)

▶ Describe and talk about what they see. (KUW: 30-50 months)

▶ Explain own knowledge and understanding, and ask appropriate questions of others. (KUW: 40-60+ months)

▶ Use talk to organise, sequence and clarify thinking. (CLL: 40-60+ months)

▶ Sing simple songs from memory. (CD: 40-60+ months)

▶ Explore colour, texture, shape, form and space in two or three dimensions. (CD: 40-60+ months)

▶ Handle small and large equipment. (PD: 40-60+ months)

Appealing creatures

Using vegetable peelers to help create unique fruit and vegetable creatures

What you need:

- ▶ Selection of fruit and vegetables for creature base, suitable for carving and peeling such as: potatoes, apples, parsnips, swede, carrots, squash or gourd, marrow, aubergine

- ▶ Small fruit and vegetables for detail such as: broccoli, raisins, grapes, small tomatoes or potatoes
- ▶ Vegetable peelers
- ▶ Pipe cleaners, toothpicks
- ▶ Knives for cutting and shaping (to be used by an adult or with adult supervision)

What you do:

▶ **Explore and talk**

▷ Together unpack the range of fruit and vegetables.

▷ Talk about the shapes, colours, textures and names of the fruits and vegetables. Listen and note if children share their experiences and preferences.

▷ Observe how the children handle them, how they describe the more unusual or unfamiliar ones such as gourds or aubergines.

▷ Do they question their peers or adults on any items they are unsure of? What language and words do they use to question?

▶ **Investigate and experiment**

▷ Explore the potential and opportunities the vegetable peelers offer. Help children to push hard with the blade whilst pulling at the same time, holding the vegetable for them may help.

▷ Investigate sculpting and digging with the end of the peeler. Explore the peelings that are created – the shape, size, smell and texture. How could we create a really long peel?

▷ You could share with children images of previously created fruit and vegetable creatures (a google search produces a wealth of images).

▷ Allow the children's imagination to run away with them as they experiment with sculpting, peeling, chopping and attaching different parts of fruits and vegetables together to create their own individual unique character.

▷ Use toothpicks or pipe cleaners to attach smaller, detailed parts to the main vegetable base.

▷ Do they gain inspiration from their prior experiences perhaps of popular culture, such as Mr Potato Head from Toy Story or maybe a favourite story character such as The Gruffalo or The Troll?

▷ Help children to create the characters that they describe. Encourage the language of shape and size: 'I wonder what shape the tail will be?' 'How could we make that? What vegetable or fruit could you use?'

Taking it further

▶ Make a label for your creature, 'I wonder what they will be called? Do they have a secret power?'

▶ Let your creature star in their own story. Use small world props, natural materials and other creatures (friends willing!) to create a creature tale.

▶ Photograph the construction of your creature. Put the photos in order and have a go at writing the instructions underneath, or scribe for children their instructions for each stage.

▶ Have a go at planting any seeds that have been discovered whilst creature creating.

And another idea...

▶ Children could create their own snack station and take responsibility for preparing the snacks from washing to peeling. Include snacks such as carrots and cucumbers that can be peeled.

▶ Use peelings to create pictures and patterns – they won't last long but could be photographed and annotated with children's descriptions.

▶ Use peelings to enhance small world play scenes such as undergrowth or a swamp!

▶ Make vegetable soup. Use straight vegetables (carrots or parsnips) for ease of peeling for younger children.

▶ Use a vegetable peeler to whittle a variety of sticks – Elder is particularly effective.

Learning and development

▶ Work creatively on a large and small scale. (CD: 40-60+ months)

▶ Explore, colour, texture, shape, form and space in two or three dimensions. (CD: 40-60+ months)

▶ Express and communicate their ideas, thoughts and feelings by using a widening range of materials, suitable tools, imaginative and role play and designing and making. (CD: 40-60+ months)

▶ Talk about personal intentions, describing what they are trying to do. (CD: 40-60+ months)

▶ Use simple tools to effect changes to materials. (PD: 40-60+ months)

▶ Practise some appropriate safety measures without direct supervision. (PD: 40-60+ months)

▶ Use talk to organise, sequence and clarify thinking, ideas, feelings and events. (CLL: 40-60+ months)

Chocolate shop

Use tongs to serve up a delicious treat in 'The Chocolate shop'

What you need:

▶ Ingredients for making chocolate play dough or salt dough (see page 80)

▶ Selection of serving tongs: BBQ tongs, sugar tongs, ice tongs and food tongs in a range of shapes and sizes

▶ Empty chocolate box inner trays

▶ Empty chocolate boxes

What you do:

▶ **Explore and talk**

▷ Talk about the selection of packaging, 'I wonder what was in them?' Encourage children to describe the shapes and sizes of the holes. Does anyone have a favourite chocolate?

▷ Share and describe chocolate memories such as hot chocolate, chocolate fountains, chocolate birthday cakes, chocolate ice cream on holiday, chocolate decorations on the Christmas tree.

▷ How would the children feel about setting up their very own chocolate shop? What would we need? What could it be called? Scribe a list of the children's ideas. How could we find or make the things that we will need? Help the children to collect the resources and props they have identified for their shop.

▶ **Investigate and experiment**

▷ Talk about the ingredients and changes in texture when making 'pretend' chocolate to use in 'The Chocolate shop' (name dependent on individual groups of children).

▷ Pretend chocolate could be created by either making, baking and decorating salt dough to represent chocolates or making chocolate play dough and sculpting and decorating it to look like chocolates – these will smell just like delicious chocolates too!

▷ Use the opportunity to explore the shape, pattern, size and decoration of various chocolates. (Collecting chocolate lists from chocolate boxes around Christmas time could be really helpful here!)

▷ Once you have set up your role-play chocolate shop, serve up your home made chocolates into chocolate trays using tongs! How easy is it to fit the chocolates in the holes? Can the children match chocolate shapes with the shape of the holes? Try out different sized tongs. Are some easier?

Taking it further

▶ Wrap the chocolate boxes in paper and ribbon.

▶ Make name labels for all of the workers on chocolate decorated paper! Laminate and string. Can they find their name?

▶ Write gift tags for the boxes.

▶ Give the chocolates a name and make labels such as 'Nice and Nutty' or 'Orange Surprise'.

▶ Introduce kitchen scales into The Chocolate shop.

▶ Provide different size cake cases from small petit four cases to large muffin cases. Introduce seasonally decorated cases to promote discussion.

▶ Make coffee play dough (see page 80) to add variety to the shop's menu and enhance children's sensory experiences and language during role-play.

And another idea...

▶ Use tongs to transport bone shaped dog biscuits into a bowl. How many biscuits can you transport in a minute or two minutes? Link with Old Mother Hubbard Nursery Rhyme.

▶ Use tongs to fill an astronaut's backpack (mini purse type) with moon rock (glass nuggets).

Learning and development

▶ Continue to be interested, excited and motivated to learn. (PSED: 40-60+ months)

▶ Use language for an increasing range of purposes. (CLL: 40-60+ months)

▶ Write their own names and other things such as labels. (CLL: 40-60+ months)

▶ Use language such as 'circle' or 'bigger' to describe the shape and size of solids and flat shapes. (PSRN: 40-60+ months)

▶ Engage in imaginative play and role-play based on their own first hand experiences. (CD: 30-50 months)

All together now!

Activities which involve using a combination of kitchen bits and pieces and a lot of noise!

What you need:

▶ Somewhere to attach utensils such as a clothes rail, tree, fence or washing line

▶ A selection of kitchen instruments to play e.g. colanders, saucepans, lids and metal jugs.

▶ A selection of utensils to use as beaters, such as, teaspoons, serving spoons, wooden spoons, wooden spatulas, plastic spatulas or whisks

▶ A large space – preferably outside!

▶ String or 'S' Hooks

I will need

What you do:

▶ **Explore and talk**

Attach the selection of kitchen utensils to the washing line and then step back and observe as the children explore the kitchen items. How do the children investigate them? Do they swing them? Do they choose an item to use as a beater? Do they unhook them and re-order them? Do they work from left to right or right to left or in a random order?

▷ Can you make really loud sounds? Why are some louder than others?

▷ Can you make really quiet sounds? What is the quietest sound that can be made?

▷ Is the wooden spoon quieter or louder than the metal spoon or plastic spatula?

▶ **Investigate and experiment**

▷ Follow the lead of you inquisitive young learners and stimulate their enquiry skills and thoughts by providing additional resources as requested or suggested. Summarise their discoveries, reiterate their thoughts and ideas or link their discoveries with those of their peers.

Taking it further

▶ Add musical accompaniments to familiar songs and rhymes.

▶ Create their own songs and rhymes, using the kitchen instruments as accompaniments.

And another idea...

▶ Use the kitchen instruments to add sound effects to stories such as 'And the Giant came tumbling down and landed with a crash!'

▶ Play conductors. Use picture clues to indicate playing slowly (a snail) or very quickly (a cheetah) or loudly or quietly.

Learning and development

▶ Explore the different sounds of instruments. (CD: 40-60+ months)

▶ Recognise and explore how sounds can be changed and sing songs from memory. (CD: 40-60+ months)

▶ Respond in a variety of ways to what they hear, see, touch, feel and smell. (CD: 40-60+ months)

▶ Make comparisons and create new connections. (CD: 40-60+ months)

▶ Practice some appropriate safety measures without direct supervision. (PD: 40-60+ months)

Hand gym fun!

Using kitchen implements to develop crucial muscles and fine motor control!

What you need:

- ▶ Spaghetti tongs, bowls or containers and cooked spaghetti or pasta shapes
- ▶ Ice tongs, ice cubes and an ice bucket
- ▶ Barbecue tongs, large sweet jars/tins and ping pong balls
- ▶ Garlic press, plates and play dough
- ▶ Juicer and lemons or oranges
- ▶ Zester, bowls and a selection of fruit
- ▶ Potato masher, play dough, salt dough, gloop, mud, thick finger paint

What you do:

- ▶ **Explore and talk**

  - ▷ Children can explore the kitchen implements.

  - ▷ Talk about familiar ones and investigate ones they haven't seen before. How do they work? What are they used for? Do you need to press or squeeze?

▶ **Investigate and experiment**

▷ Use tongs to transfer objects and materials into bowls and containers or serve food in the home corner.

▷ Use a garlic press to experiment with play dough and other malleable materials. Squeeze it through the press or make some alien hair!

▷ Use a juicer and zester to press and squeeze out the juice from different fruit – maybe making a fruity drink to share.

▷ Use a potato masher to mash and print in dough, paint and other media. Make mashed potato footprints!

Taking it further

▶ Try using other interesting objects to transfer, mash or squeeze such as seasonal vegetables.

▶ Use a marrow or mini pumpkin with pegs and hammers (much more exciting than a plastic peg board!)

▶ Make activities more challenging once mastered such as putting a ping pong ball in the water tray to fish out with tongs.

And another idea...

▶ Raid your kitchen cupboards for inspiration!

▶ Set new challenges with different implements. Using the tongs, how many acorns can you place in the ice cube tray?

Learning and development

▶ Use a range of small and large equipment. (PD: 40-60+ months)

▶ Handle tools, objects and malleable materials safely and with increasing control. (PD: 40-60+ months)

▶ Engage in activities requiring hand-eye coordination. (PD: 30-50 months)

▶ Use one-handed tools and equipment. (PD: 30-50 months)

▶ Interact with others, negotiating plans and activities and taking turns in conversation. (CLL: 40-60+ months)

▶ Manipulate objects with increasing control. (CLL: 30-50 months)

▶ Respond in a variety of ways to what they see, hear, smell touch and feel. (CD: 40-60+ months)

Rock and rolling

Using an everyday rolling pin to create unique paintings

What you need:

▶ A large space outside

▶ Rolls of lining paper or large sheets of paper (you could use the reverse of display backing paper when displays come down)

▶ Selection of rolling pins, including small wooden and plastic ones, patterned rollers used for creating prints, large rolling pins in both wood and plastic

▶ Paint trays large enough for rolling the rolling pins in

What you do:

▶ **Explore and talk**

▷ Introduce the different rolling pins. Give children time to thoroughly explore the texture, material, weight and rolling properties of the rolling pins.

▷ Are all the rolling pins the same? Why not?

▷ Have you ever seen a rolling pin being used? What was it used for?

▷ Why do some of the rolling pins have pictures or patterns on?

▷ Do they all roll? Ensure all children have time to explore pushing and rolling the rolling pins.

▶ **Investigate and experiment**

▷ Create large scale rolling pictures!

▷ Dip the rolling pins in the paint tray and push away, across the paper!

▷ Do they all roll the same way? How far will they roll? What happens when one paint trail crosses over another paint trail? Will the colours mix?

▷ Could we make them roll further? Do the paint trails remind you of anything?

Taking it further

▶ Measure the paint trails using footsteps, which is the longest?

▶ Use the ends of the rolling pins to create circular prints amongst the paint trails, making a wonderful spot and stripe effect.

▶ Guess the rolling pin: Children turn their backs, whilst one child creates a paint trail – which rolling pin was it?

▶ Explore the marks other items make when rolled – perhaps, conkers, pebbles or a variety of balls.

And another idea...

▶ Make up games which involve picking up objects by rolling Velcro hair rollers.

▶ Experience the sensation of physically rolling in large indoor or outdoor spaces.

▶ Play games involving rolling balls towards a target.

▶ Use paint rollers in a wide range of sizes from very small to large industrial rollers!

Learning and development

▶ Use increasing control over an object. (PD: 40-60+ months)

▶ Respond in a variety of ways to what they see, hear, smell, touch and feel. (CD: 40-60+ months)

▶ Investigate objects and materials by uses all of the senses as appropriate. (CD: 40-60+ months)

▶ Describe and talk about what they see. (KUW: 40-60+ months)

▶ Look closely at similarities, differences, patterns and change. (KUW: 40-60+ months)

▶ Use talk to organise, sequence and clarify thinking. (CLL: 40-60+ months)

Plunging puddle power

Making puddles disappear!

What you need:

▶ A space outside to create puddles or a nice drizzly day where there are lots of puddles

▶ Selection of sink plungers, including the type that holds water

▶ Buckets and water trays

▶ A letter with a problem... Perhaps, Angelina Ballerina wants to come and practise her dancing, but there are too many puddles and her ballet shoes would get wet. Or, Tiddles the cat would love to come and visit, but doesn't like his furry feet getting wet.

What you do:

▶ **Explore and talk**

▷ Sink plungers! What can these fascinating items do? Talk about the possibilities of these strange looking objects.

▷ Touch and smell the different materials – wood, rubber and plastic.

▷ Read the letter and the problem together. What can we do? Can we help? How?

▷ Discuss the different ideas generated.

▶ **Investigate and experiment**

▷ Children experiment with using the sink plungers to suck up and expel water.

▷ Look at the differences between the plungers, do they all suck up water?

▷ Could they suck up a puddle? Which size puddle?

Taking it further

▶ Respond to the letter with photographs, letters, drawings or maybe video clips of the children's ideas and results in removing the puddles.

▶ Use syringes as small scale plungers to fill up cups and bottles or make small puddles.

And another idea...

▶ Find other ways of sucking up water – perhaps sponges or straws.

▶ Investigate the power of expelling air from the plunger. Perhaps, create targets with empty bottles – How many can you blow over using the plunger?

▶ Label the bottles with different numbers and add up the scores.

Learning and development

▶ Talk activities through, reflecting on and modifying what they are doing. (CLL: 30-50 months)

▶ Use talk to connect ideas, explain what is happening and anticipate what might happen next. (CLL: 30-50 months)

▶ Describe and talk about what they see. (KUW: 30-50 months)

▶ Explain own knowledge and understanding, and ask appropriate questions of others. (KUW: 40-60+ months)

▶ Ask questions about why things happen and how things work. (KUW: 40-60+ months)

Post office fun!

Using weighing scales to help sort the parcels in the post office

What you need:

▶ A selection of scales – balance scales, kitchen scales, digital scales

▶ Variety of pre-wrapped parcels of differing weights

▶ Labels, stampers and other items for a post office role-play.

What you do:

▶ **Explore and talk**

▷ Observe children as they explore the range of scales. Note if children link these to prior experiences. What language do they use as they explore them?

▷ Record children's understanding of weight and weighing or numeral recognition as they are busy exploring the scales.

▶ **Investigate and experiment**

▷ In the context of the post office, investigate how to find out how heavy the parcels are.

▷ Create simple labels, such as, 'light', 'heavy' or 'very heavy' to label the parcels.

▷ Sort the parcels into sacks according to weight. Link the weight of the parcels to the prices. The heavier the parcels the more they cost to post. Set a tariff with simple prices and labels. Model and reinforce the language of weight.

▷ Follow the children's lead as they take on the various roles within the post office.

Taking it further

▶ If there is one close by, a visit to a real post office or sorting office would provide a wonderful opportunity for widening children's experiences and helping them to make sense of the world of posting items!

▶ Create a letter sizer, just like the one in the real post office, to measure, sort and price the letters according to size.

▶ Design and create different stamps. Investigate different stamp designs, especially child friendly ones, such as, Christmas editions or ones showing familiar characters.

And another idea...

▶ Create an interactive display with different scales, include a variety of numbered sacks or pouches. Set challenges for the children: Which sack is heaviest? Can you order the sacks from heaviest to lightest? Who do the sacks belong too? (Observe children's ideas and reasoning. The red sack belongs to Little Red Riding Hood or the heaviest sack belongs to The Giant).

▶ Create a health centre role-play; include scales for babies and children to be weighed.

▶ Create a vets role-play; include scales for weighing animals perhaps extend to working out food allowances based on weight, maybe small cup, medium cup or large cup according to weight.

▶ Collect items from the vegetable patch (or garden pots), weigh them to record the harvest! Or create a grocer's shop or supermarket with scales for weighing purchases.

Learning and development

▶ Show an interest in shape and space by playing with shapes or making arrangements with objects. (PSRN: 30-50 months)

▶ Begin to understand 'bigger than' and 'enough'. (PSRN: 30-50 months)

▶ Order two items by weight or capacity. (PSRN: 40-60+ months)

▶ Sort familiar objects to identify their similarities and differences, making choices and justifying decisions. (PSRN: 40-60+ months)

▶ Describe solutions to practical problems, drawing on experience, talking about own ideas, methods and choices. (PSRN: 40-60+ months)

▶ Use language such as 'greater', 'smaller', 'heavier' or 'lighter' to compare quantities. (PSRN: 40-60+ months)

Pies, potions and pancakes!

Let the imagination run wild as a range of utensils are used to create unique concoctions!

What you need:

A selection of kitchen utensils, containers and food stuffs for making concoctions.

▶ Funnels, measuring spoons, whisks, spatulas, jugs, wooden spoons, slotted spoons, fish slices

▶ Empty bottles, cake cases, bowls, empty yoghurt pots, ice cream tubs

▶ Flour, lentils, oats, rice, sugar and water.

▶ Containers which sprinkle (empty seasoning containers)

Create an inviting display and investigation area by hanging utensils around the area, perhaps theme the table with chef style black and white checked paper and create chef's hats for children to wear whilst busy creating.

What you do:

▶ **Explore and talk**

▷ Listen as children share their ideas of what they could make.

▷ Support children to talk through their ideas and identify what else could be added or other resources they might need to assist and extend their creations.

▷ Model and reinforce language appropriate to the children's direction of play and learning – recipe, ingredients, mix, stir, whisk, sticky, smooth or sprinkle.

▶ **Investigate and experiment**

▷ Get busy! A rich opportunity to observe and note children's direction of discovery, along with, the skills they demonstrate such as measuring, whisking, or transferring.

▷ Observe and note how individual children approach their discoveries. Do they know from the beginning what they are going to create? Do they enjoy the experience of exploring and experimenting, with no specific end product? Are they influenced by their peers' concoctions? Do they lead other children in the area?

▷ Make and explore different consistencies. How could it be made runnier or thicker? Which is easiest to pour? What would happen if pies were runny or soup was thick?

▷ Using a wide range of implements explore skills such as, scraping, smoothing, whisking, sieving, pouring, estimating and filling.

Taking it further

▶ Create names and labels for their creations –'Bubbly Pie' or 'Sprinkle Potion'.

▶ Make up songs and rhymes to describe actions: Whisk, Whisk, Whisk away. Whisk, Whisk, Whisk, all day.

▶ Photograph creations, along with the creator.

▶ Rotate utensils and 'ingredients' to offer different experiences and opportunities.

And another idea...

▶ How about creating an 'Imagination Station' in the outdoor area, with small and large scale containers and utensils such as buckets and large bowls. Ensure access to natural materials to mix and explore. Which utensils make the best mud pie?

Learning and development

▶ Use simple tools to effect changes to materials. (PD: 40-60+ Months)

▶ Use a range of small and large equipment. (PD: 40-60+ Months)

▶ Handle tools, objects, construction and malleable materials safely and with increasing control. (PD: 40-60+ Months)

▶ Realise tools can be used for a purpose. (KUW: 30-50 Months)

▶ Begin to try out a range of tools and techniques safely. (KUW: 30-50 months)

▶ Use simple tools and techniques competently and appropriately. (KUW: 40-60+ months)

▶ Select the tools they need to shape, assemble and join materials they are using. (KUW: 40-60+ months)

Art smart with kitchen implements

▶ Create contemporary art (small and large scale) using kitchen implements for printing. Can you guess the kitchen tool that made the print?

▶ Explore paint, gloop, mud, jelly, even custard or gravy!

▶ Add glitter, sequins, wool, string, dried pasta, lentils etc. to create different textures.

▶ Use implements to mix, stir, whisk, scrape, serve or scoop!

▶ Create 3D art with kitchen implements – thread with wool, string, ribbons, raffia, fabric strips or any other exciting materials you can find. Suspend around the setting. Link colours and textures to themes or topics perhaps blue, white and yellow for a seaside theme or hues of green for down in the jungle!

▶ Create a kitchen implement art gallery/interactive display.

▶ Design your own kitchen implement.

▶ Try colour mixing using whisks – hand whisks and electric whisks.

▶ Use a flour sifter/dredger to create large scale art. You could also try salt, powder paint, glitter, dry sand, semolina, couscous etc.

▶ Link to interests, themes and topics such as fireworks or the seasons.

Learning and development

▶ Work creatively on a large and small scale. (CD: 40-60+ months)
▶ Explore colour, texture, shape, form and space in two or three dimensions. (CD: 40-60+ months)
▶ Use imagination in art and design. (CD: 40-60+ months)
▶ Express and communicate their ideas, thoughts and feelings by using a widening range of materials and suitable tools. (CD: 40-60+ months)

Recipes

Gloop

Ingredients

▶ Cornflour
▶ Water
▶ Food colouring
▶ Fragrance of your choice

Method

▶ Mix water and cornflour to the consistency of your choice – extra runny through to thick depending on the activity.
▶ Add a colour and fragrance – yellow lemon, pink strawberry, drinking chocolate brown.

Chocolate play dough

Ingredients

▶ $1\frac{1}{4}$ cups of flour
▶ $\frac{1}{2}$ cup of cocoa powder
▶ $\frac{1}{2}$ cup of salt
▶ $\frac{1}{2}$ tablespoon of cream of tartar
▶ $1\frac{1}{2}$ tablespoons of cooking oil
▶ I cup of water

Method

▶ Mix all of the dry ingredients.
▶ Add the cooking oil and water.
▶ Stir quickly and mix well.
▶ Cook over a low heat or microwave stirring every 30 seconds, until a dough ball forms.

Salt dough

Ingredients

▶ 1 cup of salt
▶ 2 cups of flour
▶ 1 tablespoon of oil
▶ 1 cup of water
▶ Food colouring, fragrance of your choice

Method

▶ Mix all ingredients together to form a soft dough.
▶ Knead dough until preferred consistency is reached adding more flour/water as necessary.

Coffee play dough

Ingredients

▶ 4 cups of flour
▶ 1 cup of salt
▶ $\frac{1}{2}$ cup of salt
▶ $\frac{1}{4}$ cup of instant coffee
▶ $1\frac{1}{2}$ cups of warm water

Method

▶ Dissolve the coffee in the warm water in a bowl.
▶ Mix the flour and salt together, in another bowl.
▶ Make a well in the flour and salt mixture and add one cup of the coffee mixture and stir.
▶ Continue to add the remaining mixture until the dough is smooth.

If you find that the consistency of any of these recipes is too dry, simply add a few drops of water until the desired consistency is reached. If the dough is too moist, add small amounts of flour until you get the correct consistency. Storing dough wrapped in cling film, in an airtight container will prolong its life.